More AMAZING BUT TRUE SPORTS STORIES

More AMAZING BUT TRUE SPORTS STORIES

Phyllis and Zander Hollander

An Associated Features Book

SCHOLASTIC INC.
New York Toronto London Auckland Sydney

PHOTO CREDITS: 12, 16, 45, 48, 54, 63, 71, 93, 104, 107, 110, 114, 124: Wide World. Frontispiece: California Angels/SPS. 8: (left) Southern Michigan State Prison/SPS; (right) Detroit Tigers/SPS. 16: Seattle Mariners/SPS. 20: Mitchell Reibel. 30, 69: NBC-TV. 34: Kansas City Royals/SPS. 35: Ira Golden. 39: NASA/SPS. 50: Jimmie Heuga Center/SPS. 59: John Biever. 74: Notre Dame/Steven Navtatil. 80: Malcolm Emmons. 102: Hockey Hall of Fame/SPS. 116, 128: UPI: Bettmann.

ISBN 0-590-43876-X

Copyright © 1990 by Associated Features, Inc. All rights reserved. Published by Scholastic Inc.

12 11 10 9 8 7 6 5 4 3 2 1   0 1 2 3 4 5/9

Printed in the U.S.A.   01

First Scholastic printing, November 1990

CONTENTS

ACKNOWLEDGMENTS

The collection of stories in this book developed from many sources — friends who spotted the unusual, fellow sportswriters, the wire services, newspapers, and magazines. The authors especially acknowledge contributing writers Eric Compton of *Newsday* and Dave Kaplan of the *New York Daily News,* and the athletes responsible for *More Amazing But True Sports Stories.*

INTRODUCTION

The one-armed pitcher who made it to the major leagues.

The runner who outraced a bear.

The hockey goalie who scored a goal.

The cyclist who pedaled over the Aegean Sea.

The football coach who left tickets for the deceased Elvis Presley.

The catcher who subbed a potato for a ball.

The outfielder who was arrested when his throw killed a sea gull.

Bizarre? Startling? Strange? Unexpected? It all happens in *More Amazing But True Sports Stories*, assembled by the same team that produced *Amazing But True Sports Stories*.

In this collection of 76 stories covering a wide range of sports, you'll get to read about heroes and villains, miracles and hoaxes, courage and comebacks.

And you'll meet the boxer's mother who jumped into the ring and belted her son's opponent.

All amazing, but true!

— *Phyllis and Zander Hollander*

More AMAZING BUT TRUE SPORTS STORIES

Courage, determination and all-around athletic ability made Jim Abbott a major leaguer.

BASEBALL

Surprising the Handicappers

Admittedly nervous, Jim Abbott came to the California Angels' spring training camp in Mesa, Arizona, in March 1989.

He was only 21 years old, straight out of college. And he had never faced big-league hitters before.

But he welcomed the challenge because life for him has always been an extra challenge.

Abbott was born without a right hand.

As a child growing up in Flint, Michigan, Abbott learned to play baseball the same way many kids do: playing catch with his father in the backyard. Yet kids can be cruel. Many made jokes about his birth defect, calling him nicknames like "Stub." But the jokes and nicknames didn't last long.

Abbott became the best in the neighbor-

1

hood — in all sports. "He was going to show everybody," said Mike Abbott, his father.

Mr. Abbott watched his son spend countless hours throwing a ball against a brick wall and then mastering a technique to throw and catch. When he threw, the stub of his right hand would be stuck in the pocket of his glove. Then he'd move his left hand into the glove and make the catch. Next, tucking the glove under his right arm and, with the ball in his left hand, he'd be ready to throw again.

Jim's athletic spirit and left arm developed quickly. In his debut as a high-school quarterback at Flint Central, he threw four touchdown passes and led his team to the state semifinals.

But baseball was his favorite sport. Jim continued to work at overcoming his handicap. He taught himself to hit, gripping the bat with his left hand and steadying it with his right forearm. He batted .427 in his senior year. And his pitching motion and glove switching became fluid, almost like a magician's sleight of hand.

Abbott attended the University of Michigan, where he won 26 games and lost only eight in three seasons. Then he pitched the U.S. team to the baseball gold medal at the 1988 Olympic Games in Seoul, Korea. For his performances in '88, he received the Sullivan Award as the nation's most outstanding amateur athlete.

But the Angels' selection of Abbott as the eighth choice in the draft raised many eyebrows. People said politely that they admired Abbott's courage, but a one-handed pitcher could never survive against major-league competition.

"I never thought of it as a handicap," Abbott said. "If people wouldn't keep reminding me, I'd never think about it."

In 1989, he answered all the nay-sayers. The promising southpaw became a regular member of the Angels' starting rotation and won 12 games. He lost 12. He posted a 3.92 earned-run average, largely with a two-pitch repertoire — a fastball that gets up to 93 miles an hour and a slider.

"It was a tough year. It was a long year. But it was a great year," Abbott said of his first major-league season, in which he became the most closely watched and celebrated rookie in many years.

Oh, What a Relief!

Jeff Reardon accepts his lot in life with no complaints. He's a fireman, the one who puts

3

out the flames when the starting pitchers are in trouble.

He's done it so effectively that in 1989 he was named the Rolaids Reliever of the Decade following a career that began in 1979 with the New York Mets and has taken him to Montreal, Minnesota and Boston.

Going into the 1990 season, he had appeared in 647 major-league games and he'd never started in any of them.

The Sea Gull Tragedy

It started out as just another game in Toronto — the Blue Jays vs. the New York Yankees, on August 4, 1983.

With the Yankees on the field before the Blue Jays were to bat in the fifth inning, Yankee outfielder Dave Winfield was completing his warm-up tosses. He threw the ball toward the batboy and it hit and killed a sea gull.

While the dead bird was removed from the outfield, the fans booed and threw rubber balls at Winfield. But that wasn't the end of it.

After the game, Winfield was arrested by Toronto police and charged with cruelty to animals. He was booked and released on $500 bail.

The newspapers had a field day. One Toronto headline blared: "Damn Yankee Charged in Slaying of Seagull in Ballpark." And the *New York Post* read: "Winfield Murders Seagull; Faces 6 Months as Jailbird."

"All I can tell you," said a sheepish Winfield, "is it's unfortunate one of the fowl of Canada is no longer with us. It wasn't intentional."

"If they're going to say it was deliberate, you should see the throws he's made," said Yankee manager Billy Martin. "It's the first time this year he's hit the cutoff man."

Despite the presence of thousands of witnesses, a lifeless victim and the perpetrator in hand, the prosecuting attorney dropped the charges because they wouldn't fly.

Like Father, Like Son

The no-hitter is considered the ultimate one-game achievement for a pitcher, whether in the major leagues, the minor leagues, Little League, or any other league.

Nolan Ryan's five no-hitters (four with the California Angels, one with the Houston Astros) are the most ever in the majors. There have also been brothers with no-hitters (Bob

Forsch, St. Louis Cardinals, and Ken Forsch, Houston Astros). How about a father and son?

On January 6, 1973, Urbano Lugo threw a no-hitter for Caracas against La Guaira in the Venezuelan League. Fourteen years later, on January 27, 1987, Urbano Lugo, Jr., duplicating his father's performance, tossed a no-hitter for Caracas against La Guaira — the same teams as in 1973.

If that wasn't coincidence enough, the man who caught father and son in both games was Bo Diaz, who has played in the major leagues with the Red Sox, the Indians, the Phillies and the Reds.

From Prison to the Big Leagues

He wore number B115614. He was one of 4,000 convicts in Southern Michigan State Prison in Jackson, Michigan. And he was just a teenager.

The crime happened in early 1970. Ron LeFlore, then 17, and two companions tried to get some easy money one night. With LeFlore carrying a gun, they held up a check-cashing booth in a Detroit ghetto.

"I never even knew how much we got," he said. "We had the money in a bag and left the scene. We got into a cab, but a police car started following it and they got us. I think the store had an alarm to the police station."

Once in prison, LeFlore began looking for a way to pass the time. One day, he decided to try out for the softball team, even though his only baseball experience was pickup games on playgrounds. Although raw in fundamentals, he could run like a deer. And he could hit.

In 1973, Billy Martin, then the Detroit Tigers' manager, visited the prison to conduct a baseball clinic and met LeFlore. Martin convinced the prison officials to arrange a furlough for a day's tryout with the Tigers. And on his 21st birthday, LeFlore had a tryout at Tiger Stadium.

The Tigers were impressed. "He has tremendous natural ability," said Detroit scout Bill Lajoie. "He's . . . well, I'd say the fastest runner I ever clocked. He's got a very strong arm and a lot of power."

Two weeks later LeFlore was paroled and the Tigers assigned him to their Clinton, Iowa, farm team.

Less than 13 months later, on August 1, 1974, in Milwaukee's County Stadium, Ron LeFlore was batting leadoff for the Detroit Tigers.

"It was beyond my wildest dreams," he

Ron LeFlore in prison (left) and as a Detroit Tiger

said. "I never had any idea I'd become a professional ballplayer."

In 1976, he hit in 30 consecutive games and played center field on the American League All-Star team. In 1978, he led the league with 68 stolen bases. He wrote his autobiography, *Breakout*, and was the subject of a television movie, *One in a Million*, in which actor LeVar Burton played LeFlore. He played five seasons with the Tigers before joining the Montreal Expos and the Chicago White Sox.

"Coming out of prison into baseball," Ron LeFlore said, "was like going from death to life. I was very lucky."

Long Live the Ball!

On June 29, 1913, in Cincinnati, umpire Hank O'Day was given three new balls before the start of the game between the Chicago Cubs and the Cincinnati Reds.

O'Day threw one to the Reds' starting pitcher, Leon Ames, and, as it turned out, the game was a free-swinging affair. The teams combined for 20 hits and 15 runs as the Reds prevailed, 9–6.

When it was over, O'Day handed back two of the balls while Johnny Kling, the Reds' catcher, carried the *game ball* off the field.

Incredible as it may seem today — when dozens of balls are used in a game — the Cubs and Reds played the entire game with just one ball.

This Spud's for You

Catcher Dave Bresnahan was hitting .149 for Williamsport, Pennsylvania, in the Eastern League and his was not a household name even though his uncle, Roger Bresnahan, had made the Hall of Fame as a catcher for the New York Giants and the Chicago Cubs.

But the 25-year-old Bresnahan was determined to make his mark on baseball. On the day of a night of a doubleheader on August 31, 1987, against Reading, Bresnahan went to the supermarket and bought a bag of potatoes. In the locker room, with help from his teammates, he peeled and rounded the potatoes and stuck one of them inside an extra catcher's mitt.

He obviously had a plan. And he put it into execution in the fifth inning of the first game when there was a Reading runner on third, with two out. He called time out, telling the umpire that he had problems with his mitt. He proceeded to the dugout and picked up the mitt with the potato in it.

The pitcher, who was in on the act, responded to Bresnahan's signal for a slider, low and away. Bresnahan caught the ball with his glove hand, then took the potato from his bare hand and intentionally fired it over third-baseman Oscara Mejia. The base-runner, Rick Lundblade, taking advantage of the wild throw, broke for home. But when he got there, Bresnahan was waiting to tag him with the ball.

"When I tagged the runner," said Bresnahan, "the umpire looked stunned and called time out."

Meanwhile the Williamsport left fielder retrieved the potato as Bresnahan's teammates roared with laughter.

The umpire, Scott Potter, not only called the runner safe, but he threw Bresnahan and his potato out of the game. Bresnahan was fined $50.

Soon after, the Cleveland Indians, Williamsport's parent team, released him.

"Everybody thought it was funny except the umpire and Cleveland management," Bresnahan said.

But the promotional people in Williamsport were pleased enough with his half-baked stunt to have a Potato Night for the team's final home game. Usually tickets cost $2.75, but fans could get in by paying $1 and bringing a potato.

Two bushels of potatoes were collected and Bresnahan signed each one, "This spud's for you."

The Century Mark

It was the day before Christmas, December 24, 1989, and there was stirring about. It was the 100th birthday of Paul F. (Bill) Otis, and guests and residents at the Jensen Nursing Home in Duluth, Minnesota, were honoring

One-time major leaguer Paul Otis celebrated his 100th birthday in 1989.

the oldest former major-league player.

Otis, a graduate of Williams College, was an outfielder who had played only one month in the majors, in 1912 — four games with the New York Highlanders (predecessors to the New York Yankees). He remembers his only hit — off the Washington Senators' Hall of Famer Walter Johnson — in 20 at-bats.

He wound up in the minors and a broken ankle ended his short career.

Otis still has his glove and Highlander cap.

The Earthquake Series

There was a buzz of excitement in San Francisco's Candlestick Park on October 17, 1989. The San Francisco Giants were about to play their Bay Area rivals, the Oakland A's, in Game 3 of the World Series.

Oakland had won the first two games, but the fans who poured into the stadium on this late Tuesday afternoon were in a cheering, festive mood. A band was playing on the field. Hundreds of balloons were set to be released as Candlestick Park prepared for its first World Series game in 27 years. In just 21 minutes, the first pitch was to be thrown.

But at 5:04 PDT, Candlestick Park rolled and trembled. At first, some thought it was fans in the upper deck stomping their feet. But the Giants' Will Clark, who was doing some pregame jogging in the outfield, said, "I knew something was wrong when the ground was moving faster than I was."

Baseball commissioner Fay Vincent was standing in front of his seat, near the dugout. "The ground started to shake," he said, "and I shook with it."

ABC was doing its pregame television show when announcer Al Michaels said, "There's an earth — " and the picture was lost.

The first-ever Bay Area World Series was rocked by the first-ever World Series earthquake.

It lasted 20, maybe 30, seconds. A strange quiet hushed over the crowd. Players, fans, and umpires alike were dazed and confused. And frightened. "When I realized it was an earthquake and not a little earthquake, it was scary," said umpire Al Clark. "I don't think I've ever been more scared in my life."

The light towers rocked back and forth. A section in Candlestick's upper stands in right field cracked and pieces of concrete fell. Fortunately, nobody was seriously injured.

Then, one by one, the players went into the stands to find their families. Wanting to get the crowd safely out of the powerless stadium, commissioner Vincent called off the game and ordered the stadium evacuated.

Soon the word spread that northern California had been ravaged by the earthquake, that highways and bridges had collapsed, that homes and lives were destroyed.

Suddenly, in the dark quiet of Candlestick Park, baseball did not seem so important.

There were those who felt the Series should be cancelled. But it resumed ten days later, and the A's went on to sweep the Giants, 4–0.

All in the Family

Baseball has always been a family sport. The family can watch it and the family can play it.

In the big leagues, there have been notable brother combinations — pitchers Dizzy and Daffy Dean, with the St. Louis Cardinals; outfielders Joe, Vince, and Dom DiMaggio; pitchers Jim and Gaylord Perry, who won more than 500 games between them; and Ken and Bob Forsch, the only brothers to pitch no-hitters.

Then along came the Griffeys. Both outfielders, Ken, Sr., was 37 and playing with the Atlanta Braves when the Seattle Mariners chose Ken, Jr., as their top pick in the 1987 amateur draft. Before the 1989 season began, Ken, Sr., signed as a free agent with the Cincinnati Reds, while his son had an invitation to the Mariners' spring-training camp.

Seattle planned to take a look at the 19-year-old Griffey, but figured he would need at least another season of minor-league ball. But Junior batted .360 in spring games and a few days before the season opened, manager Jim Lefevbre called him into his office and told him he had made the team. Ken, Jr., immediately called dad to give him the good news.

On a day off with the Cincinnati Reds, Ken Griffey, Sr.,
watched son Ken, Jr., play for the Seattle Mariners.

The younger Griffey quickly showed that he belonged in the majors. He doubled in his first official at-bat. A month later, he hit two home runs to help the Mariners beat the Yankees. With his speed, power and defense, he became a fan favorite in Seattle and was so popular by midseason that a local company made a chocolate bar with his name on it.

An injury slowed down the youngster late in the season, but he still finished with 16 home runs, 64 RBI and a .246 average. Meanwhile, dad, in his 19th season, had 8 homers and 30 RBI, and hit .263 with the Reds.

If this had been a movie, the scriptwriters would have had the Griffeys on opposing teams in the World Series.

But it was historic enough for the first father and son playing at the same time in the majors.

Making Her Pitch

Women's sports have come a long way in the past 20 years. Women's professional tennis and volleyball, and college basketball, have all gained in popularity due to exposure on national television, and in schools across the country, girls now play sports that were once thought to be only for boys. Back in 1931, however, virtually every sport was dominated by men, and that's what makes Jackie Mitchell so special.

Mitchell, 17 years old, was a left-handed pitcher signed by the Double-A Chattanooga Lookouts as a publicity stunt. Lookouts owner Joe Engle had seen Mitchell pitch in a local game and thought he could boost attendance by announcing that she would pitch in an exhibition game against the New York Yankees on April 2, 1931.

These were the Yankees in their heyday, featuring a Murderers Row led by Babe Ruth, Lou Gehrig and Tony Lazzeri.

The Chattanooga starter gave up two hits at the beginning of the game, so Lookouts manager Bert Niefhoff brought in Mitchell. Even though it was only an exhibition, she officially became the first woman to play in a professional baseball game.

The first batter she faced was the great Babe Ruth. Imagine him batting against a 17-year-old girl! But Mitchell got ahead of Ruth, 1-and-2, with three sinkers, and then threw a fastball past him for a called third strike. Ruth threw his bat away in protest as the crowd cheered.

Now it was Gehrig's turn. A sinker for strike one. Another sinker, strike two. Then a third. Gehrig swung and missed. All Mitchell had done as the first woman to pitch in professional ball was to strike out two of the greatest sluggers in history. After she walked Lazzeri, Niefhoff pulled her from the game and she left to an ovation from the crowd.

That would be Mitchell's only chance against big leaguers. She continued to play semipro baseball in Chattanooga and would always treasure the memory of the day she struck out the Mighty Babe and Larrupin' Lou.

Long Distance

Jake Neely didn't bring his baseball glove with him, but maybe he should have. When Neely, a Toronto Blue Jays fan, bought his ticket to Game 4 of the Blue Jays-Oakland Athletics American League playoffs at the Toronto SkyDome on October 7, 1989, he found that the seat was in Section 540 — far out in left field and in the uppermost deck of the gargantuan new stadium.

Neely could barely make out the action on the field when Oakland slugger José Canseco came to the plate in the third inning. Blue Jays left-hander Mike Flanagan threw a strike and then a pitch on the inside part of the plate. Canseco swung, and drove the ball high and deep to left field. Toronto left fielder Mookie

Oakland's Jose Canseco hits 'em out of sight.

Wilson took one look and realized he had no chance. The ball landed in Neely's lap in Section 540.

Though the SkyDome computer estimated the length of Canseco's home run at 480 feet, many press-box observers and most players guessed that ball traveled well over 500 feet and ranked as one of the longest home runs ever hit.

The New York Yankees' Mickey Mantle holds the unofficial record for the longest homer with a 565-foot drive off Chuck Stobbs of the Washington Senators in Washington's old Griffith Stadium in 1956. Mantle also had two homers that ricocheted off the facade of the upper deck at Yankee Stadium, drives that baseball people estimated at 525 to 550 feet.

Even though teammates were impressed by Canseco's homer — Rickey Henderson called it "unbelievable" and Dave Parker, a 16-year veteran, said it was the longest he'd ever seen — Canseco wasn't overwhelmed. "I just missed it," he said. "I've got to get hold of one tomorrow."

As for Neely, he was reminded of what his friend said to him as they got to their seats at the start of the game. "You didn't bring your glove," the friend said. "If one gets hit up to us, we're out of luck."

Returning Home

Southpaw Frank Viola made the headlines in 1987 when he led the Minnesota Twins to the World Championship over the St. Louis Cardinals. He was named World Series' Most Valuable Player.

The masterful Viola went on to win the Cy Young Award in 1988 as the American League's No. 1 pitcher. Midway in his eighth season with the Twins, his only major-league team, came the stunning news: Viola, a native of Long Island, New York, had been traded to the New York Mets for five pitchers.

That gave him a unique distinction: first pitcher to be traded the year after winning a Cy Young Award.

Two for the Price of One

It was the late spring of 1984, and Tom Seaver was wrapping up his magnificent career. The right-handed pitcher was closing in on his 300th career victory. He had already notched Hall of Fame credentials — five 20-win seasons, three Cy Young Awards, a no-hit game, a 19-strikeout game and a World Series ring with the 1969 New York Mets.

Now Seaver was with the Chicago White Sox and, at age 39, was the club's best pitcher.

The White Sox were playing the Milwaukee Brewers on the night of May 8 when the scene was set for Seaver to reach another milestone. As the scheduled starter the following night, he was sent home to rest while the White Sox and the Brewers were in the early innings.

So Seaver went to bed while the two teams went into extra innings. When neither team could break the tie, the game was suspended after 17 innings and scheduled for completion the next night.

When the game resumed, Seaver relaxed in the White Sox's clubhouse as the teams played through the 18th, 19th and 20th innings. When it went into the 21st, Chicago pitching coach Dave Duncan came into the clubhouse and told Seaver, "Get your stuff on. We're gonna need you."

Seaver got into uniform, went down to the bullpen and started warming up. In the 25th inning, Seaver was called in. He was hit hard, but held the Brewers scoreless, thanks to a catch at the wall and a double-play grounder. "I went to the dugout and was putting my jacket on — I'm not even facing the field — and I hear this crack," Seaver recalled. "Harold Baines hits the first pitch over the center-field fence. It's the only game I ever won in relief."

Seaver's night had just begun, though. He started and won the second game, 5–4, and thus became one of the few pitchers in baseball history to win two games in the same day. "I called my wife afterward and she said, 'How did the team do?' I said, 'We won, we won.' Then she said, 'How did you do?' I said, 'I won, I won.' "

The Battle Back

Jim Eisenreich seemed different from the other kids in St. Cloud, Minnesota. He appeared nervous and would often twitch and shake.

One day, during a Little League game, when he was about eight, his father called him over. "What's wrong with you?" he asked. "Why are you making those faces?"

Jim got very confused and cried. "I didn't know what he was talking about," he said later. "I thought, heck, I can't help it. I'm not trying to do it."

Jim Eisenreich played outfield and had a strong arm. He also had a terrific batting stroke. By the time he got to college at St. Cloud State, he was a standout.

But his condition was still a mystery. From time to time, Jim suffered from tics, which would leave him hyperventilating and shaking on the playing field. When he got up to the major leagues with the Minnesota Twins in 1982, the problem persisted. He went to numerous doctors, hypnotists and psychotherapists. Some said Jim's strange behavior resulted from "stage fright" at being in the big leagues.

Fans in other ballparks, after seeing Jim shake, cruelly taunted him. And the problem worsened. During a game in Boston, he ran off the field, charged into the clubhouse and tore off his uniform in total disgust.

The same thing happened at a game in Milwaukee.

Then he left baseball.

Finally, a doctor correctly diagnosed Jim's problem. He had Tourette syndrome, a neurological disorder that can never be fully cured, although its symptoms can be minimized with proper medication.

After two years out of baseball, Jim returned to the big leagues with the Kansas City Royals. In 1989, at age 30, he got a chance to play regularly because of injuries to other players, and he made the most of it.

Jim played all 3 outfield positions and led the Royals in batting with a .293 average, in doubles with 33 and in stolen bases with 27.

He even beat out Bo Jackson as Kansas City's Player of the Year.

More importantly, he proved he could handle his disability.

A Commissioner's Odyssey

It seemed like an innocent college prank.

Somebody locked 18-year-old Francis T. (Fay) Vincent, Jr., in his dormitory room at Williams College in the winter of 1955. But Vincent, a big, strong freshman, had an idea. He would crawl out the window and walk on the ledge to an adjacent room.

Unfortunately, the ledge was icy. Vincent slipped and fell four stories to the ground, crushing two vertebrae.

His spine had to be rebuilt using a bone from his hip. Vincent spent almost a whole year in bed, in a body cast. During his recovery, he passed the time listening to baseball games on the radio and watching them on television.

Vincent would never be able to play baseball. He had little use of his legs and was forced to use a crutch for balance. "I had to learn to walk all over again," he said.

But Vincent worked hard to overcome his disability. He became a successful businessman and a movie studio executive. Then, in

1989, his close friend and new baseball commissioner Bart Giamatti asked Vincent to become his deputy commissioner — sort of like a vice president for baseball.

Six months later, Giamatti died suddenly of a heart attack. Baseball was devastated by the loss of the popular new commissioner — and especially saddened was Vincent.

In the past, the naming of a new commissioner was a lengthy process. But baseball's 26 club owners were impressed with Vincent's qualifications and performance in the short time he had served.

They named him commissioner to replace his friend on September 13, 1989. "I have a great sense of conflict," he said, "because I know this is not the way to get the job."

It was, indeed, a strange twist of fate for Vincent, who, 35 years earlier, had developed his passion for baseball while listening and watching games as he recovered from his terrible fall.

The Balk Man

There was no reason to think that the Texas Rangers-Toronto Blue Jays exhibition game on March 7, 1988, would be anything special. After all, exhibition games, especially early in

March, are events where veterans play just enough to break a sweat — they pitch a few innings, take a few swings at the plate, field a few grounders — and then let the rookies trying to make the club take over.

A veteran pitcher such as the Rangers' Charlie Hough viewed the game as an opportunity to get his arm ready after a winter away from baseball. What Hough got was a rude introduction to a new season.

During the off-season, commissioner Peter Ueberroth, in an attempt to give base-runners more of an edge, had told umpires to enforce the balk rule to the letter of the law. Pitchers would have to come to a complete stop in their windup before delivering the ball to the plate. In this way, runners on base would have a better idea of exactly when a pitcher would be throwing to the plate.

Hough always had an unusual motion when runners were on base. Instead of bringing his hands down to his belt, he would keep them chest-high, a few inches away from his body. Umpire Dan Morrison decided to let Hough know early in spring training that he would have to change this motion. Morrison called Hough for an incredible nine balks in three innings, with seven of them called in one inning.

Hough, who had been playing profession-
ally for 22 seasons, was stunned. "I've seen a
lot of strange things," the knuckleballer said,
"but nothing like this."

The umpires lightened up a bit in the regular
season, and Hough was called for a total of 10
balks.

A Sportscaster's Overtime

Vin Scully, the popular voice of the Dodgers
since 1950 and a longtime NBC network announcer on baseball and golf, will long remember the weekend of June 3–4, 1989.

On a Saturday afternoon in St. Louis, he
called NBC's nationally televised Cubs-
Cardinals game, which went 10 innings. Day's
work done? Not nearly.

Minutes after the game, Scully took a private
jet to Houston for a Dodgers-Astros night
game. "We landed at 7 P.M.," Scully said. "By
the time I got there, they were playing the
national anthem and I was able to say, 'Wel-
come to the Astrodome.' "

Seven hours later, he was still in the broad-
casters' booth. The game lasted 22 innings,
ending in the wee hours of the morning with
the Astros finally winning, 5–4.

Scully got to his hotel room at 4:20 A.M.

Vin Scully has been calling them for the Dodgers for 40 years.

There would be another game at the Astro-dome that afternoon. No rest for the weary.

He was on the job that day, as always, when the Astros' Craig Biggio hit a two-out, ninth-inning home run to tie the game. Scully thought, *I can't believe it. We're going to have more baseball.*

It became a 13-inning game, with Houston winning, 7–6.

In 27 hours, Scully had broadcast 45 innings of three extra-inning games in two cities!

A MIXED
BAG

Bo's Dream Come True

November 30, 1987, Los Angeles — Monday Night Football. L.A. Raiders vs. Seattle Seahawks. Bo Jackson celebrates his 25th birthday with a 91-yard touchdown run and leads the Raiders to a 37–14 victory.

July 11, 1989, Anaheim, California — The first inning of the 60th annual All-Star Game. The batter: Bo Jackson of the Kansas City Royals. The pitcher: Rick Reuschel of the San Francisco Giants. Second pitch, Jackson swings and rockets a 448-foot home run over the center field fence at Anaheim Stadium.

Bo Jackson thrives in two worlds, baseball and football, and fulfills what history says is an impossible dream.

There are only a handful of athletes who have played both sports in the major leagues, but none have excelled in both. Not even Jim Thorpe, the Sac and Fox Indian who was called "the greatest athlete in the world" by Sweden's King Gustav V after he won the decathlon at the 1912 Olympics. Thorpe starred later in football for the Canton Bulldogs and other teams in the NFL, and was a mediocre-hitting outfielder in the majors for six years.

But Jackson defies tradition and those who said it couldn't be done.

As a schoolboy in Bessemer, Alabama, Jackson couldn't make up his mind which sport to play. He was a pitcher in baseball and would hit 20 home runs in 25 games. He was a track star, and set the Alabama prep decathlon record. Football, strangely enough, may have been his worst sport. He was rated only the fourth-best halfback in the state.

He was offered $220,000 by the New York Yankees when he graduated from high school. One of ten children in a family whose mother worked as a domestic, he rejected the offer. "I had a scholarship to college," he said, "and

Bo Jackson is a menace at bat for the Kansas City Royals.

Jackson's speed and power add up to big yardage with the Los Angeles Raiders.

I could play football, baseball and track at the same time. Plus, I could get my degree. So it was like I could get four things for the price of one, and I excelled at all four."

Leading his multi-sport achievements at Auburn University was the Heisman Trophy, which the 6-foot-1, 220-pound Jackson won in 1985. What followed was a tug-of-war for his services between football's Raiders and baseball's Royals. He wound up playing for both.

Each team prefers that he stick to one sport. Because of baseball, he can't join the Raiders until October each season, but they settle for what they can get from Bo.

He has captured the nation's imagination with his awesome feats. And he has been paid accordingly: $1.356 million by the Raiders in 1989, and $585,000 by the Royals in 1989.

Computer Chess

Gary Kasparov was a chess wizard. The 26-year-old Soviet had defeated hundreds of challengers to become the world champion and highest-rated player in the history of chess.

No one could beat him.

But could a computer?

Nobody knew until October 22, 1989, when Kasparov played Deep Thought, the world computer chess champion, in New York. Created by five scientists at Carnegie-Mellon University in Pittsburgh, Deep Thought had the capability to scan 720,000 possibilities a second — immeasurably faster than the human mind.

Nonetheless, Kasparov was confident. "I can't visualize living with the knowledge that a computer is stronger than the human mind," he said. "I had to challenge Deep Thought for this match, to protect the human race."

Kasparov chose the black pieces and played carefully and precisely to build a superior position. After Kasparov's 52nd move, the computer surrendered. In the second game, Deep Thought quit after 37 moves.

"I expected it," Kasparov said. "It's a great player, but without position and experience."

Time to Take the Boots Off

In a typical 90-minute soccer match, players have been known to total as much as seven miles running up and down the field.

But the NCAA championship game between UCLA and American University on December 15, 1985, was anything but typical.

Both teams were locked in a battle that night in the Seattle Kingdome, with neither able to score a goal after 90 minutes of play.

Under the rules in a tie game, the teams play a 10-minute overtime period. If there is no score in the first overtime, they play another 10-minute overtime. After two overtimes, the next overtime and any thereafter calls for "sudden death," meaning the first team to score is the winner.

Nobody scored in the first overtime. It went into a second overtime . . . then a third . . . a fourth . . . a fifth . . . a sixth . . . a seventh. Still no score.

Prior to the eighth overtime, UCLA assistant coach Steve Sampson pleaded with his weary players: "Guys, let's just get out there and finish this thing so we can go home."

With 3:55 left in the eighth overtime, a seldom-used sophomore named Paul Burke broke through American's defense and booted a shot from 13 yards to beat the goalie.

The marathon was over! UCLA had won the championship in the longest soccer game in collegiate history — an exhausting ordeal that ran almost two full games, lasting a total of 2 hours, 46 minutes, and 5 seconds.

Pole-Vaulting to the Moon

The President of the United States was on the telephone. It was a long-distance call from

It was one giant leap to the moon for Buzz Aldrin.

Washington, D.C., to the Sea of Tranquility on the moon.

President Nixon: "Hello, Neil and Buzz. I am talking to you from the Oval Room at the White House. And this certainly has to be the most historic telephone call ever made. I just can't tell you how proud we all are of you . . . Because of what you have done, the heavens have become a part of man's world. . . ."

The day was July 20, 1969. Minutes before, Colonel Edwin E. "Buzz" Aldrin, Jr., had exclaimed, "Beautiful, beautiful," as he stepped on the moon's surface, the second man in history to do so. The first, only minutes earlier, had been Neil Armstrong.

Whether on earth or literally "out of this world," Buzz Aldrin early in life had shown signs of knowing where he was going and how to get there.

Sports had always been a big part of his life, and at Montclair High School in New Jersey, he excelled not only in academics, but also in football and pole-vaulting.

In the summer of 1947, he went off to West Point, New York, home of the U.S. Military Academy. Too small at 5-foot-9 for varsity football, he concentrated on pole-vaulting — that is, when he wasn't studying. As a vaulter, he soared to a top height of 13 feet, 8 inches — at a time when fiberglass poles, like trips to the moon, were not yet fashionable.

Aldrin graduated third in his class in 1951 and went on to win his Air Force wings. Eighteen years later, the ex-pole-vaulter and his companions took the greatest leap of all mankind — to the moon.

Marathon Dip

She didn't do her swimming in a pool where Olympic gold medals are won and where sunbathers find relief from the heat. When Diana Nyad took a dip, it was in the ocean for hours at a time.

In marathon swimming, overcoming adverse conditions can be as rewarding as reaching one's destination. On August 20, 1979, Nyad had the pleasure of doing both. She outlasted the strong Gulf Stream currents, mountainous waves, sharks, and jellyfish stings to become the first person to swim from the Bahamas to Florida.

Twenty-seven hours and 38 minutes after leaving North Bimini, the 30-year-old New Yorker was saluted by the whistles of welcoming boats as she swam ashore at Juno Beach, Florida.

Her left eye was swollen shut from saltwater, and the coating of latex she used to protect her from Portuguese men-of-war was in shreds. But there was an ocean-wide smile on her face. Only two weeks earlier, she had failed to make the same crossing, falling victim to jellyfish stings after 12½ hours.

Although the distance in a straight line from North Bimini to the Florida coast is 60 miles, Nyad's trainers estimated she swam nearly 89 miles because of strong currents that tugged at her.

Mastering the Channel

He was only 11 years old and was facing a challenge that had defied many an adult: swimming across the English Channel.

England's Thomas Gregory entered the waters at Cape Gris-Nex, France, on September 5, 1988, and embarked on the 21-mile swim. Eleven hours and 45 minutes later, he crawled ashore in Dover, England.

He was the youngest person ever to swim the English Channel.

Cycling in the Air

According to mythology, Daedalus escaped from the island of Crete and flew to Greece with wings made of wax and feathers. But his son, Icarus, never made it. He flew too close to the sun, and as the wax of his wings melted, he plunged into the sea and drowned.

Some 3,500 years later, on April 23, 1988, a Greek named Kanellos Kanellopoulos decided to emulate Daedalus' flight.

Was he crazy? Could a man turn myth into reality?

Kanellopoulos was undaunted. The 30-year-old cycling champion and member of the Greek Olympic team believed he could use his legs and a light tailwind to pedal his fragile aircraft, called *Daedalus 88*, over the Aegean Sea.

As he took off from Crete and ascended into the air, Kanellopoulos looked like a giant dragonfly. He kept pumping his legs as he cruised above the azure waters of the Aegean. Nearly four hours and 74 miles later, Kanellopoulos gracefully floated down to the Greek island of Santorini.

He had flown from myth to reality!

"It is a triumph for science, for man and for history," declared Kanellopoulos. "We have revived the myth and have discovered a new means of travel between the islands."

Ageless Wonders

Josef Galia of West Germany, Dr. Paul Spangler of San Luis Obispo, California, and Noel Johnson of San Diego, California, had something in common when they lined up for the start of the New York City Marathon on November 5, 1989.

They were the only 90-year-olds in the race!

Galia, the oldest at 91 and a retired automotive engineer, was running his 15th marathon. He didn't run in his first one until he was 76. For Spangler, a retired surgeon, this was his 11th marathon. Johnson, a onetime boxer and aircraft mechanic, ran his first New

York City Marathon when he was 80. And he is the author of *Living Proof: I Have Found the Fountain of Youth*.

How did they do in the grueling 26-mile race? Galia was the only member of his age group to finish. His time was 6 hours, 43 minutes, 21 seconds. There was no record of when Johnson dropped out, but Spangler lasted 19 miles and complained that he had been tired out by "giving too many interviews before the race."

The winner, Tanzania's Juma Ikangaa, was timed in 2:08:01.

Comeback on Wheels

In 1986 Greg LeMond did what no American had ever done — win the Tour de France, the world's longest, toughest and most celebrated bicycle race.

The Nevada native covered nearly 2,000 grueling miles over a course that included stretches of the Alps and Pyrenees and became the first non-European victor in an event first held in 1903.

But nine months after his triumph, LeMond almost lost his life. While on a hunting expedition in the Sierra Nevada foothills, LeMond was accidentally shot in his right side and back when his brother-in-law fired at a wild turkey

With the Arc de Triomphe in the background, Greg LeMond rides down the Champs Elysees on the way to victory in the Tour de France.

in heavy brush. The shotgun pellets broke two of LeMond's ribs, piercing his intestines, liver and kidney. Near death, he was taken by police helicopter to a hospital in Sacramento, California, where surgeons removed many of the pellets but had to leave a number of them in his back and legs.

His recovery was slow and painful. "I'd pace the room and just cry because it hurt so much," he said. "The shooting covered such a large part of my body and I had such a long incision that I didn't have any energy until several weeks after I got home."

Eventually, LeMond began to regain his strength. But after starting a training program, he was felled again, this time by an emergency appendectomy. And the next year LeMond underwent a shin operation.

Although he was unable to compete in the Tour de France in 1987 and 1988, he was determined to race in 1989. Few thought he had much of a chance, considering his injuries and the punishing 21-day event that included dizzying alpine climbs in oppressively hot weather.

Going into the race's final stage — a 15-mile leg between Versailles and Paris — LeMond trailed leader Laurent Fignon of France by 50 seconds. "Greg believes he can win," Fignon had said on the eve of the last leg, "but it is impossible. I am too strong in the mind and the legs. Fifty seconds is too much to make up in such a short distance."

Undaunted, LeMond completed the 15 miles in a record 26 minutes, 57 seconds (averaging 34 miles per hour) and defeated Fignon by eight seconds — the narrowest margin of victory in the history of the race.

His courage and incredible comeback were so impressive that *Sports Illustrated* named him the 1989 Sportsman of the Year.

"It's a miracle for me," LeMond said. "To think that two years ago, I was almost dead."

Outrunning the Bear

Nancy Pease of Anchorage was leading the women's field in the 1989 Crow Pass Crossing — an Alaskan wilderness run — when she encountered a female black bear and her two cubs.

"The cubs dashed off, but the mama bear rushed me," Pease told *USA Today*. "She closed within ten yards. My first instinct was to wave my arms and shout at her. You're not supposed to run because they think you're prey. But I ran. I was looking for trees. Fortunately, the bear stopped."

There were 10 miles to go in the 26 ½-mile run and the 27-year-old Pease turned up her speed. She was determined to lose the mama bear.

Meanwhile, some of the others in the field of 115 saw a wild boar and they, too, turned on the juice. But none of the women moved as swiftly as Pease, who wound up winning her fifth consecutive Crow Pass crown in 3:28:58.

Bill Spencer of Indian, Alaska, was the over-

Jimmie Heuga slaloms to a bronze medal in the 1964 Olympic Games.

all winner in 3:05:25, but he didn't have to contend with a bear.

Meeting the Challenge

He was a world-class skier, a member of the U.S. Ski Team for a decade. And the record shows that when he was 21, Jimmie Heuga earned a bronze medal in the slalom in the 1964 Olympic Games at Innsbruck, Austria. He was just seconds behind fellow American Billy Kidd, who took the silver.

They were the first U.S. athletes to win medals in Olympic alpine skiing. Heuga would later become the only American male to win the prized Arlberg-Kandahar in Garmisch, Germany. But Jimmie's is a tale that goes far beyond the slopes he conquered.

At the peak of his career, in 1970, Jimmie was diagnosed as having multiple sclerosis (MS), a disease that short-circuits the nervous system. He was urged to live a quiet and tranquil life. At that time, MS sufferers were advised that physical activity would worsen their condition.

"Like most of the others," says Jimmie, "I followed that advice. But I began to have less energy, feel unhealthy and unmotivated. I deteriorated physically and mentally."

In 1976, he decided to take charge of his life. He developed a program of stretching and strengthening exercises. He took up bicycling and had to devise pedals that would keep his spastic feet from sliding off. He learned to safely crash his bike at the end of his ride because of his balance problems.

He swam and skied again, using a self-taught method to compensate for his ongoing coordination problems. But his goals went beyond helping himself. He spent three years working with the National Multiple Sclerosis Society, and from this experience has estab-

Despite multiple sclerosis, Heuga now cycles, swims and skis.

lished the nonprofit Jimmie Heuga Center in Vail, Colorado, which is dedicated to "reanimating the physically challenged."

At the Center, people with MS learn positive attitudes, methods for functioning more effectively in day-to-day life and exercise routines tailored to them by a staff of doctors and physiologists.

Jimmie is not cured; there is no known cure for MS. His resolve, however, is to lead a full and active life, and to help others like him improve the quality of their lives.

Jimmie continues to defy the odds. His wife Deborah, whom he married in 1986, gave birth to a 7-pound, 8-ounce boy, James Wilder Heuga, in July 1989.

"Neon Deion"

Flashy and cocky, he is known as "Neon Deion" and "Prime Time." He inspired the nicknames as an All-America defensive back at Florida State University.

Deion Sanders had more than football credentials. His all-around athletic ability appealed to the New York Yankees and they signed him to a minor-league contract in 1988. Suddenly, he was in demand in two sports.

The Atlanta Falcons made him the No. 5

pick in the NFL draft in June 1989, when he was already playing baseball in the minors.

While contract talks with the Falcons were going nowhere, Sanders was playing outfield for Columbus (Ohio) in the International League. In late summer of '89, the Yankees brought him up to the majors and, despite his inexperience, he got a chance to start in the outfield. On September 5, he rapped his first home run, against the Seattle Mariners.

But the following day, Sanders' agent reached an agreement with football's Falcons, and Sanders left the Yankees to join Atlanta for its NFL season opener on September 10 against the Los Angeles Rams.

With little preparation, having missed training camp and the preseason games, Sanders didn't figure to play much, if at all. But Falcon coach Marion Campbell inserted him in the lineup as a punt returner. On his first return, he picked up 15 yards, and on the next one he electrified the crowd by speedily snaking his way to a 68-yard touchdown return.

He thus became the first in history to hit a home run in the majors *and* score a touchdown in the NFL in the same week.

FOOTBALL

Best in the Clutch

Twelve-year-old Joe Montana was sitting on his aunt's porch waiting for dinner. He was starving because he had been playing baseball all day and hadn't had a bite to eat.

When he got to the table, he became dizzy. Then he fell backward and passed out.

It wouldn't be the last time Montana hyperventilated.

Growing up in football-crazed western Pennsylvania, Montana's primary sports were baseball and basketball. He didn't start playing quarterback for his high-school football team until midway through his junior year.

Montana attended Notre Dame, but never played a full football season due to a series of injuries. He even sat out an entire year due to a broken collarbone.

For Joe Montana it is one comeback after another.

But injuries didn't keep him from becoming a master of the comeback, first as a collegian and then as a pro. In 1975 against Air Force, he rallied Notre Dame from a 30–10 deficit with 10 minutes left to achieve a 31–30 victory.

His last game for Notre Dame, the 1979 Cotton Bowl against Houston, defied belief. A freak ice storm in Dallas made the playing field like a skating rink, and at halftime, Montana developed hypothermia; his body temperature dropped to 96 degrees.

At first, the team doctor refused to let him go out for the second half. But Montana gulped down two cans of hot chicken soup, and his temperature returned to normal. Back in the game, he proceeded to rally the Fighting Irish from a 34–12 deficit to a 35–34 triumph as he threw a touchdown pass on the final play of the game.

Continuing his magic with the San Francisco 49ers, in 1980, he sparked what many call the greatest comeback in NFL history — a 38–35 victory over the New Orleans Saints after the 49ers trailed, 35–7, at the half.

In a 1982 playoff game against the Dallas Cowboys, he culminated a last-minute drive with a touchdown pass to Dwight Clark that propelled the 49ers to their first Super Bowl.

Again, in January 1989, he came through in Super Bowl XXIII against the Cincinnati Bengals. With over 75,000 in the stands at Miami's Joe Robbie Stadium and more than 100 million watching on television, the 49ers trailed, 16–13, with three minutes to go and the ball on San Francisco's eight-yard line. Montana came very close to passing out.

"Between all the excitement and having to yell so loud to call signals, I used all my air," Montana would say later. "I hyperventilated. Everything got blurry and I thought I was going to faint. It took forever before it cleared."

When it did, Montana completed eight of

nine passes, capped by a 10-yard strike to John Taylor with 34 seconds to go. That gave the 49ers a 20–16 verdict.

Montana and his teammates made sure there would be no need for a comeback effort when they met the Denver Broncos in Super Bowl XXIV on January 28, 1990, at the Louisiana Superdome in New Orleans.

Montana threw a record five-touchdown passes and won the Most Valuable Player Award for the third time as the 49ers demolished the Broncos, 55–10.

The cool quarterback had done it again.

A Ticket for Elvis

Coaching a pro football team is serious business, but Jerry Glanville likes to lend a touch of comedy to lighten the load.

In 1988, as the leader of the Houston Oilers, Glanville made it a practice to leave tickets to Oiler games for Elvis Presley, James Dean and the Phantom of the Opera.

It all added up to good publicity, a host of Presley and Dean look-alikes and, of course, unclaimed tickets.

Glanville had his fun, but discontinued his deceased-celebrities offer in 1989. He was fired after the '89 season and soon after took over as coach of the Atlanta Falcons. The fans in Atlanta hoped he'd give them not only a winning team, but also more of his Presley-and-Dean routine.

The Fog Bowl

The date was December 31, 1988. The scene was Soldier Field in Chicago. There were over 65,000 people watching the Chicago Bears play the Philadelphia Eagles in an NFC divisional playoff game.

But most of them barely saw it.

With two minutes left in the first half, fog rolled in from nearby Lake Michigan. It enveloped Soldier Field, making visibility nearly impossible — even on television.

At one point, Terry Bradshaw, the former Pittsburgh Steeler quarterback who was broadcasting the game for CBS, described a play: "He runs right . . . out of sight."

Dozens of pro football games have been played in blizzards. Many have been played in driving rainstorms. And others have been played in bone-chilling cold, most notably in January 1982 in Cincinnati when the wind-chill factor dropped to 59 degrees below at the Bengals-Chargers American Conference championship game.

But fog had never so affected an NFL game as it did in "The Fog Bowl" in Chicago that day.

"I couldn't see the quarterback where I was," Bears coach Mike Ditka said. "I don't know how the players could see."

But according to referee Jim Tunney, the players *could* see — at least just enough for the game to continue.

And it did, as the Bears went on to defeat the Eagles, 20–12. "It was," said a fan named Tom McKee, seated in Soldier Field's upper deck, "the best game that I've never seen."

The Refrigerator

It happened so fast. Before anybody knew what to think and before anybody envisioned the consequences, Chicago Bears coach Mike Ditka had slipped a rookie defensive tackle into his offensive backfield against the Green Bay Packers. On national television.

It was Monday night, October 21, 1985, and, in a sense, this was the birth of 314-pound William "The Refrigerator" Perry.

Twice in the first half, Ditka replaced veteran fullback Matt Suhey with Perry near the goal line. And twice Perry delivered crushing blocks on an unfortunate Packer linebacker

William (The Refrigerator) Perry scores on a pass in his rookie season as a Bear.

named George Cumby. Both times Walter Payton scored a touchdown. But in between, Perry got his chance as a ballcarrier and he responded by bursting off right tackle for one yard and a touchdown.

He celebrated with a thunderous spike in the end zone and ABC announcer O. J. Simpson said Perry looked like Marcus Allen.

The Bears beat the Packers, 23–7, on their way to a Super Bowl crown with an overnight hero who rocked the Richter scale.

Two weeks later, Perry caught a touchdown pass against the Packers, sparking another round of Perrymania. He appeared on *Late*

Night with David Letterman. Johnny Carson was next in line. Fan clubs sprouted up across the country. He inspired an instant book and there were numerous editorials ("Stop That Refrigerator!" said the *Washington Post*).

The columnists kidded him. "What Mike Ditka did with William Perry was the best use of fat since bacon, the highest calling for a refrigerator since the first ice cube," wrote Ray Sons in the *Chicago Sun-Times*.

The good-natured Perry laughed louder than anybody — and all the way to the bank. The public loved their gentle giant. Soon "The Refrigerator" was simply "Fridge." By mid-season, the normal $300 appearance fee paid to Bear rookies had skyrocketed to $5,000 for the 22-year-old South Carolinian, one in a family of 12 children.

For heroics and acclaim, he would never be able to match that rookie season of 1985.

In and Out of the Spotlight

He was a 23-year-old substitute teacher — in Latin, French, physical education, auto shop, mechanical drawing, anything — at his old school, Lakeland Regional in Wanaque, New Jersey. He was making only $36 a day and lived with his in-laws.

After school, he helped out Lakeland's varsity football team as an assistant coach. But at just 5-foot-7, he was smaller than most of the students he coached and was often mistaken for a student.

Nothing came easy for Eric Schubert. He had always dreamed of going to a big-time college and becoming a kicker in the NFL. He went to the University of Pittsburgh and made the team as a walk-on. He was a good placekicker. Then, in his senior year, in 1983, Schubert kicked off against Syracuse and his foot hit the newly painted insignia on the field, dislocating his right kneecap. He was not chosen in the NFL draft.

He signed with the Pittsburgh Maulers of the United States Football League, but the team folded a week before he got married. He also tried out for the New Jersey Generals of the USFL and the New England Patriots, but he was cut.

In late October 1985, New York Giants kicker Ali Haji-Sheikh was injured and the club needed a replacement. Coach Bill Parcells called the Schuberts' in-laws' house to see if Eric could come in for a tryout. "Oh, no," Michelle Schubert, Eric's wife, told Parcells. "The little son-of-a-gun is out buying a lottery ticket."

"I guess she thought it would terminate the deal," Parcells said later. "But Eric called back five minutes later."

Schubert passed the tryout. And on November 4, against the Tampa Bay Buccaneers before over 72,000 fans and a network television audience, Eric Schubert kicked five field goals into a swirling wind — at distances of 24, 36, 24, 41 and 33 yards — to lead the Giants to a 22–20 victory. He became an instant sensation.

Good Morning America interviewed him. Reporters from newspapers around the country called and announcers from three New York television stations drove to his house for interviews. He was chauffeured into Manhattan for a live spot. *Sports Illustrated* informed him he was their NFL Offensive Player of the Week. And the soap opera *Days of Our Lives* booked him for a role.

In the span of one week, Schubert had gone from a $36-a-day substitute teacher to a $3,700-a-week full-time professional placekicker.

But it didn't last for long. He was cut by the Giants prior to the next season. He caught on briefly with the St. Louis Cardinals in 1986 — only long enough to kick three field goals in 11 attempts and 9-for-9 extra points.

And so ended the brief NFL career of Eric Schubert.

What a Deal!

Rarely a day goes by without a player or two being traded. It's all part of the business of sports, the constant goal to improve a team's chances of winning.

However, fans in Dallas and Minneapolis in particular and around the nation, were shocked on October 11, 1989, when they heard the terms of the trade involving Dallas Cowboys' running back Herschel Walker, the two-time Pro Bowl selection and 1982 Heisman Trophy winner out of Georgia.

Herschel Walker finds a new home with the Minnesota Vikings.

The Cowboys sent Walker to the Minnesota Vikings in exchange for running back Darrin Nelson, linebackers Jesse Solomon and David Howard, cornerback Issiac Holt, defensive end Alex Stewart, and seven future draft choices.

Never in the history of sports has one player been traded for 12.

Dream Team

Jerry Croyden picked up the phone in his office and dialed *The New York Times* in great excitement. As publicity man for Plainfield Teachers College, he was calling in the results of the school's latest victory. This time he reported that Plainfield had beaten Ingersoll, 13–0.

The rewrite man at the *Times* took the score and in the next day's paper, the victory became a matter of record. This meant the third triumph for unbeaten Plainfield, whose previous victims had been Winona (27–0) and Randolph Tech (35–0).

During this 1941 season, Plainfield was on its way to a record that in some respects would be unequaled in the annals of college football.

The star of the team was a Chinese sophomore halfback, John Chung, who averaged 9.3

yards a carry as Plainfield went on to win its first six games. In one publicity release, Croyden explained: "The prowess of Chung may be due to his habit of eating rice between the halves."

But suddenly, things went wrong at Plainfield. On November 13, publicist Croyden sent out what proved to be his final press release: "Due to flunkings in the midterm examinations, Plainfield Teachers has been forced to call off its last two scheduled games with Appalachian Tech tomorrow and with Harmony Teachers on Thanksgiving Day."

It was an abrupt finish for John Chung, who had accounted for 69 of Plainfield's 117 points, and for a team that might have been invited to one of the smaller Bowl games on New Year's Day. But it was understandable in light of the surprising story that appeared in the November 17 issue of *Time* magazine.

"For three weeks running," the account read, "the sports page of *The New York Times* has dutifully recorded the football victories of Plainfield (N.J.) Teachers College. The Philadelphia *Record* and other papers also took occasional notice of unbeaten Plainfield Teachers. The only error in all the reports . . . was that Plainfield and its opponents were nonexistent."

There was no Plainfield, no John Chung, no rice, no victories. Caswell Adams, a sportswriter on the New York *Herald Tribune*, filled in the details of the great hoax. He discovered that the ghost team and its star halfback were dreamed up by a group of stockbrokers at Newburger, Loeb & Co., a Wall Street brokerage firm. The chief instigator was Morris Newburger, an imaginative 35-year-old football fan.

Morris Newburger was Jerry Croyden. So were some of Morris' associates. On Saturday afternoons they would take turns calling the newspapers and manufacturing press releases about the marvelous feats of Plainfield.

For the stockbrokers, this was certainly no money-making proposition. It was an investment in fun and fantasy. They wanted a winning football team and they got one.

They also received a tribute, which Morris Newburger would always prize. It was a song written by the *Herald-Tribune*'s Adams to the tune of Cornell's "High Above Cayuga's Waters":

> *Far above New Jersey's swamplands*
> *Plainfield Teachers' spires*
> *Make a phantom, phony college*
> *That got on the wires*

Perfect record made on paper
Imaginary team!
Hail to thee, our ghostly college,
Product of a dream!

The Snowball Effect

The San Francisco 49ers' Matt Cavanaugh awaited the snap from center. He was the placekick holder for Ray Wersching in a *Monday Night Football* game against the Denver Broncos on November 11, 1985.

Suddenly, a snowball splattered just in front of Cavanaugh at Mile High Stadium and he bobbled the snap. He tried to scramble, then tossed a pass that was incomplete.

The 49ers were behind, 14–3, just before halftime, and Denver eventually won, 17–16. So the aborted field goal was a factor.

Who threw the snowball? The *San Francisco Examiner* offered to pay $500 for the story if the culprit would come forward. And he did. But the paper agreed to keep his name secret because he feared retaliation, including the loss of his parents' season tickets to Bronco games.

The young man expressed his apologies to the 49ers and their fans, but refused the $500.

Barefoot Kicker

Placekicker Rich Karlis of the Minnesota Vikings has a yellow tube of ointment on which it says, "For Horses — Small Animals."

He uses it for softening the skin on his right foot, the one he kicks barefoot with. He started barefoot kicking at the University of Cincinnati and the salve has served him well during a professional career that began with Denver in 1982.

After seven seasons he was released by the Broncos, but the Vikings signed him in 1989 and he had his most memorable day on November 5 against the Los Angeles Rams.

The barefoot kicker booted seven field goals in a 23–21 overtime victory. He tied the 22-year NFL record of St. Louis' Jim Bakken and broke the record for most field goals in a game without a miss.

Bakken's kicking shoe is on display at the Football Hall of Fame. Karlis' bare foot will not be on display.

A First on the Tube

At the time, not even the participants could appreciate the historical significance of the occasion.

The date was September 30, 1939, when Eu-

Skip Walz was the announcer at the first football game on television.

rope was at war, a new LaSalle V-8 automobile cost $1,200 and dinner at a fancy New York restaurant cost a dollar. On that day, in a football game played at Randalls Island in New York, Fordham overpowered Waynesburg, 34–7.

Disregarded by the crowd of 9,000 as well as by the teams, were two simple television cameras and a crew of eight. Yet this game would prove to be the start of a new era in sports, marking the first telecast of a football game.

The pioneer network was NBC, and the

game reached approximately 500 TV sets over RCA's experimental station, W2XBS.

The players said later that they had no idea the game was being televised, but the memory remains vivid for Skip Walz, who was the announcer. "I got $25 for the game," he recalled. "I did it with no monitors, no spotters, and no visual aids of any kind. This was flying blind at best. It was up to the cameraman to somehow follow my commentary, and that got particularly sticky late in the game when the light got bad."

Three weeks later, on October 22, the first professional football game was televised, with the Brooklyn Dodgers beating the Philadelphia Eagles, 23–14, at Brooklyn's Ebbets Field.

The Magic Flutie

Boston College had fought gamely against highly favored Miami and its All-America quarterback Bernie Kosar. But this one seemed to be over. Some reporters began typing their stories: "Miami beat Boston College, 45–41 . . ."

It had been a great quarterback duel: the 6-foot-5 Kosar vs. BC's 5-foot-9 Doug Flutie.

The grass field at the Orange Bowl in Miami on the evening of November 23, 1984, was

Boston College's Doug Flutie looks for receiver Gerald Phelan in the storied game against Miami.

drenched from a driving, windblown rain. But it hadn't hampered either quarterback.

Flutie had started with a flourish, completing 11 straight passes for a 14–0 lead. Kosar counterpunched with a streak of 11 completions to tie it up. But this was only the prelude to a wild game that would bring Miami's Hurricanes to a 45–41 lead with six seconds to go, BC's ball on the Miami 48.

Time for one last play.

"We didn't think we were out of it," said BC fullback Steve Strachan. "We had Doug Flutie in the huddle."

The nimble, brainy Flutie called for a play

they called "Flood Tip," in which Gerald Phelan, Flutie's roommate, would somehow reach a ball thrown into the end zone and tip it to a teammate. As it happened, the play didn't work out exactly that way.

Miami's Jerome Brown put a fierce rush on the little quarterback as time was running out. In a last-gasp heave, Flute threw the ball over 60 yards to Phelan, who seemed lost in a maze of Hurricanes in the end zone. As the ball came down, CBS's Brent Musburger went into mild hysterics: "It's . . . CAUGHT! . . . I don't believe it."

Phelan's catch of Flutie's pass gave BC a stunning 47–45 victory.

"Maybe Miami didn't think Doug could throw that far. But I knew. I've been with him for four years," said Phelan. "For a little guy, Doug throws like a giant."

Lights On!

Thomas Alva Edison never played football, but his was an illuminating presence at Galt, Canada, on the night of September 18, 1886, when the Victorias of Toronto played the Galt Football Club.

Thanks to Edison, the inventor of the light bulb, this marked the first night football game in history, according to historian Dick Lamb.

The earliest indoor game between college elevens took place in 1893 at, of all places, a riding academy in Chicago. The horses were in their stables as Chicago defeated Northwestern, 22–14, on a shortened field.

The first regularly scheduled college game played outdoors under the lights was held October 5, 1900, in Des Moines, Iowa. Drake University beat Grinnell, 6–0.

The lights were on again the following week when host Drake routed Iowa State Normal (now the University of Northern Iowa), 50–0. Iowa State Normal claimed their abnormal performance was due to lack of experience under the lights.

For the Want of a Towel

The Heisman Trophy wasn't at stake for Notre Dame's Tim Brown when the Fighting Irish met Texas A&M in the Cotton Bowl on January 1, 1988. Brown had already been named winner of the 1987 Heisman as college football's most outstanding player.

But the game would be Brown's finale and he, like his fellow seniors, wanted to leave on a winning note. Texas A&M had its own incentives, and with the exception of wide re-

Notre Dame's Tim Brown was on his way to the Heisman Trophy.

ceiver Brown's 17-yard touchdown reception, the Aggies' defense kept frustrating Notre Dame.

On one kickoff return late in the game, Brown was piled up by a horde of Aggies. When he emerged, he discovered that someone had swiped the towel that hung from his pants. Moments later, he spotted Aggie defender Warren Barnhorst proudly displaying the towel. Brown raced across the field and tackled Barnhorst in order to retrieve it.

The move cost the Irish 15 yards on a personal foul penalty. Notre Dame coach Lou Holtz benched Brown for the remaining few plays of the game. By then it didn't matter. Texas A&M won, 35–10, but Brown got back his towel.

Return of the Dropkick

The dropkick is something out of the distant past, so Pat Harmon was shocked when he noticed that the winning points in an Ohio scholastic football game in 1986 came on a dropkick.

Harmon is the historian-curator of the College Football Hall of Fame, and, indeed, his investigation verified that Rick Rice dropkicked a field goal to give Blanchester a 9–6 victory over Ross.

Harmon estimates that this may have been the first time in at least 50 years that a game at any level — high school, college or professional — was decided by a dropkick.

In the old days, when dropkicks were commonplace, Montana State freshman Forest Peters dropkicked 17 field goals in a 1924 game against Billings (now Rocky Mountain College). That's a record that will never be broken.

Three years later, a dropkick would have an impact on the rules of the game. In a 1927 New York State high-school game, New Rochelle played Yonkers and was without its star, Bill Morton. He was injured and didn't suit up for the game. Instead, he sat in the stands.

At a crucial point, the New Rochelle captain, Vin Draddy, called time and summoned Morton out of the bleachers. Morton, dressed in street clothes and wearing street shoes, dropkicked a field goal to win the game.

That sent the rules committee into action. They wrote a rule that says anybody who plays in an organized football game must wear a football uniform.

A Gift from Nigeria

Growing up in Lagos, Nigeria, Mohammed (Moe) Elewonibi (pronounced Elewon-EE-bi) excelled at soccer and also played basketball. The son of a Canadian mother and Nigerian naval officer, he moved to Kamloops, British Columbia, when he was 11 years old. He competed in a wide range of sports during his school years — but he never played football.

After high-school graduation, he worked as a lumberjack and bouncer, for which he certainly had the fitting physique (he would grow up to be a 6-foot-5, 290-pounder).

But Elewonibi wanted a college education, and the coaches at Snow Junior College in Ephraim, Utah, were so impressed with his athletic and academic potential that they gave him a scholarship and introduced him to football. Elewonibi became the star of Snow's offensive line.

Elewonibi then went on to Brigham Young University, where as a senior guard in 1989 he emerged as a powerful leader and pass-blocking lineman. In recognition of his performance, he was selected by the Football Writers Association of America as winner of the Outland Trophy, which is given annually to the nation's No. 1 collegiate lineman.

It was a remarkable achievement for the young man from Nigeria who didn't play football until he was 18 years old.

Holding the Sticks

DeWitt Clinton High School, in the Bronx, New York, has had such distinguished graduates as actors Burt Lancaster and Douglas Fairbanks, Sr., and playwright Neil Simon. How about Bernie Sherman?

Sherman played left end on the Clinton football team. He was so attached to the team that the season following his graduation in 1934, he returned to the field to hold the yardsticks at Clinton games. He has never given them up. Through the 1989 season, he hadn't missed a game — 507 consecutive games — with the 10-yard sticks.

The 75-year-old Sherman, who works for the New York State Department of Labor, says he has outlasted 15 coaches and 11 principals during his 55 years working the sticks.

And although he'll never achieve the fame of Lancaster, Fairbanks or Simon, he has become a celebrity in his own right. He has been hailed in Ripley's "Believe It or Not," and has made it into the *Guinness Book of World Records*.

BASKETBALL

Wilt's Biggest Surprise

They started calling him "Wilt the Stilt" in high school. At seven feet tall, he dwarfed opposing players and averaged 37 points a game in three years at Philadelphia's Overbrook High.

Wilton Norman Chamberlain was one of the most publicized high-school basketball players in history. He went from Overbrook to Kansas University, where he played only two varsity seasons before dropping out to join the Harlem Globetrotters for a season.

He hadn't been happy in the college game. "I was being tied up in little mob scenes around my pivot position," he said. "Two, three, sometimes four men were guarding me. By guarding, I mean they were climbing up and down my seven-foot frame and shoving

Wilt Chamberlain towered over the game . . . and here over Milwaukee's Lew Alcindor (later Kareem Abdul-Jabbar).

me around like people crowding into a subway train."

It didn't get easier for him when he joined the Philadelphia Warriors in the NBA in 1959. But he rose high above all opposition. In the 1961–62 season, he averaged an incredible 50.4 points a game. On March 26, 1962, in a game against the New York Knickerbockers, he scored 100 points!

In the course of a 14-year career with the Warriors (Philadelphia and San Francisco), the Philadelphia 76ers and the Los Angeles Lakers, Chamberlain led the NBA in rebounding 11 times and in scoring seven times. And in 1968, he became the first center in history to top the league in assists.

A perennial all-league and All-Star team selection, Wilt Chamberlain was named the league's Most Valuable Player four times.

When he retired at the end of the 1972–73 season, he had played in 1,045 games. And the most amazing feat of all was that he never fouled out in a game!

Hero for a Day

Team managers in high school and college sports get to earn varsity letters for pumping up balls, transporting gear and doing dozens of other unsung chores.

But for Dennis Hopf, manager of the Clemson University basketball team, life will never be quite the same as a result of what happened to him on January 29, 1989.

That was the day he suited up as a reserve player against Duke University because six team members had been suspended for violating academic study hall rules.

With Hopf, the Clemson Tigers had a total of seven players in uniform for the away game, and it was obvious that they would be no match for Duke's Blue Devils.

Duke rolled up the score, and with two minutes left, Clemson coach Cliff Ellis sent Hopf into the game. Unbelievably, the Duke fans cheered him.

Hopf traveled while driving through the lane for his first shot, and his second shot was blocked. Duke wound up winning, 92–62, but Hopf became the story of the game.

"When I got out of the shower," he related, "there were reporters waiting to talk to me. I was the last one out of the locker room. The coach had to come back and get me. He said, 'We've got a plane to catch.'

"I told the coach he made my fantasy come true. I've always dreamed of getting dressed for a Clemson game. I never dreamed of playing. It's a Cinderella story: Boy gets a chance of a lifetime."

When the plane landed in Clemson, South Carolina, Hopf was still the team manager. He carried the bags from the plane.

But he'd become a celebrity, if not a superstar. Cable News Network named him Player of the Day, he made the front page of *USA Today*, and he did a number of interviews with radio and television stations.

He knew it would never happen again. But for Dennis Hopf, his one touch of glory would last forever.

Points by the Bushel

The defense rested its case on January 31, 1989, when Loyola Marymount met United States International in a basketball game in Los Angeles.

The name of the game was offense. After 40 minutes of nonstop action, Loyola Marymount had defeated United States International, 181–150, in the highest-scoring game in National

Collegiate Athletic Association history.

The winners' 181 points were also the most ever by an NCAA team, and United States International's 150 points were a record for a losing team.

The teams attempted 5.6 shots per minute and averaged 8.3 points per minute.

By comparison, the NBA record for most points in a regulation game is 318 — Denver 163, San Antonio 155, in 1984.

Roadblock Ahead!

Steve McGlothin, New Mexico State's starting center during his sophomore and junior years, was a spectator at a World Basketball League game in the summer of 1988.

His program number was chosen in a random drawing that gave him the opportunity to win a new car if he made a halfcourt shot during halftime proceedings.

"I'd never made a halfcourt shot. I'd never even made a three-pointer," McGlothin said.

So he went out and split the cords with a perfect shot. And he won the car.

But two weeks later, the National Collegiate Athletic Association said he won the car with his athletic ability — which of course is true — and as a result was in violation of the rules.

He could keep the car or his senior year of eligibility, but not both, the NCAA said.

Reluctantly, he took the car back to the dealer.

Friendship Before Victory

It was a breakthrough when the national basketball team of the People's Republic of China agreed to a 1978 tour of the U.S. following the World Games in Argentina.

The chief object of curiosity for Americans was China's 7½-foot center, Mu Tieh-chu, who became known as "The Great Wall of China." His big moment off the court came when he met former NBA superstar Wilt Chamberlain in Los Angeles and got his autograph.

On the court, China lost its first three games to UCLA, San Francisco and Wake Forest. Then, Mu Tieh-chu's team surprised Georgetown, 75–69, and headed for the final game of the tour against Rutgers at New York's Madison Square Garden.

It took place on November 18, 1978, and the Chinese made their everlasting mark on the American sports scene. The score was tied at 84-all when the buzzer sounded, ending regulation time.

While an announcement was made that the

traditional five-minute overtime period would begin shortly, the Chinese players gathered their gear and walked off the floor.

Tsien Chen-hai, the Chinese coach, offered a simple explanation: "Why should we keep on playing? We're here on a friendly visit and winning or losing is not important."

Fur Real

Cameron Wilson was a promising nine-year-old basketball player in Wichita, Kansas, and he enjoyed watching the games at Wichita State University.

As a halftime promotional stunt, the university randomly chose two fans at each game to take shots for prizes. Wilson was one of the choices at a game in December 1989.

He made a layup and a jump shot from the free throw line, and then he hit from behind the three-point line at the top of the key, winning a fur coat.

He still had a chance for the big one — an automobile given for a successful halfcourt shot. But he missed it. Poor lad, he had to settle for the fur coat.

The Heater Was On

It was a cold, snowy night on January 26, 1960, in West Virginia.

It was the perfect night for a Heater.

The Burnsville High basketball team had developed a plan for Danny Heater, a 6-foot senior, to help him get a college scholarship. They would keep giving him the ball against Widen High and hope he would score enough points to break the state record.

In the game's first few minutes, Heater didn't respond. "I didn't go along with the plan at first because we've always been taught team ball," Heater said. "Then the coach called a time-out and chewed me out."

Heater got the message. Heater also got hot. Very hot. He scored 50 points in the first 16 minutes, helping Burnsville to a 75–17 lead at halftime. In the third quarter, he broke the then-West Virginia scoring record of 74 points.

"After I broke it, I wanted to come out," Heater said. But the coach kept him in the game. So Heater scored 55 points in the game's final 10 minutes as Burnsville won, 173–43.

Overall, Heater made 53 of 70 shots, mostly layups, and 29 of 41 free throws for 135 points! Not only was it a state record, it was also a national record.

"It was so unreal," Heater said later. "It was a once-in-a-lifetime game. I don't know how I did it."

Heater got his scholarship — to the University of Richmond — but he never finished his first year. He injured his back in an automobile accident and, after his parents' house burned down, he left school.

He became an airline ticket agent in Washington, D.C. Although his basketball career ended abruptly, he'll never forget that cold night in 1960 when he caught fire for 135 points. "I still get the clippings out once in a while," he said. "I think about it most during the basketball season."

Caught in the Switch

Is it possible to play for both teams in the same NBA game?

The date was March 23, 1979, and the Philadelphia 76ers were hosting the New Jersey Nets in a game that had actually begun on November 8, 1978.

Philadelphia had seemingly won the November 8 game, 137–133, but Larry O'Brien, the NBA commissioner at the time, upheld a Nets' protest of a third technical foul called by referee Richie Powers on both forward Bernard King and coach Kevin Loughery. Under NBA rules, only two technical fouls could be called on any player or coach.

O'Brien ordered that the game be replayed on March 23 from the point prior to the third technical assessed against King.

In the interim, however, four players had switched uniforms. On February 7, New Jersey traded Eric Money and Al Skinner to Philadelphia for Harvey Catchings, Ralph Simpson and cash.

When the game resumed, with Philadelphia leading 84–81 with 5:50 to go in the third quarter, the 76ers went on to win, 123–117.

None of the four players had much bearing on the outcome. Catchings fared the best, contributing eight points and four rebounds for the Nets after failing to score as a 76er in the original game. Simpson didn't score for the Nets after scoring 10 for Philadelphia, and Money had four points for Philadelphia after scoring 37 points and contributing a team-high nine assists for the Nets in the first game. Skinner didn't play in either contest.

"I remember looking at the box score the next day and seeing my name for both Philadelphia and New Jersey," said Catchings. "It was kind of weird, to say the least."

Indeed, in this one game it was possible to play for both teams.

ORIGINAL GAME

PHILADELPHIA 137, NEW JERSEY 133 (OT)

NEW JERSEY	FG	FT	Pts.	PHILADELPHIA	FG	FT	Pts.
King	3–11	2–2	8	Erving	9–25	6–8	24
Washington	7–14	4–6	18	B. Jones	4–6	2–2	10
Johnson	3–6	4–4	10	C. Jones	6–9	1–1	13
Money	15–26	7–12	37	Cheeks	1–7	0–0	2
Williamson	17–28	8–9	42	Collins	10–23	7–7	27
Elliott	0–1	0–0	0	Bibby	4–10	3–4	11
Boynes	1–4	0–0	2	Dawkins	8–10	1–2	17
V. Breda Kolff	5–7	0–0	10	Mix	6–17	5–6	17
Jordan	0–3	2–3	2	Simpson	5–7	0–2	10
Bassett	2–2	0–0	4	Bryant	3–7	0–0	6
Skinner	Did Not Play			Catchings	0–1	0–0	0
Totals	**53–102**	**27–36**	**133**	**Totals**	**56–122**	**25–32**	**137**

New Jersey ... 38	32	27	22	8	6	—	133
Philadelphia... 21	41	37	20	8	10	—	137

Rebounds: New Jersey 58 (Johnson 16), Philadelphia 55 (Erving 14); Assists: Philadelphia 42 (Bibby 10), New Jersey 26 (Money 9); Steals: Philadelphia 13 (Collins, Simpson 3), New Jersey 9 (Money 4); Blocked Shots: New Jersey 10 (Johnson 8), Philadelphia 6 (C. Jones, B. Jones 2); Officials: Richie Powers, Ed Middleton, Regan McCann; T: 2:30. A: 11,363.

REPLAYED GAME

PHILADELPHIA 123, NEW JERSEY 117

NEW JERSEY	FG	FT	Pts.	PHILADELPHIA	FG	FT	Pts.
King	3–11	2–2	8	Erving	11–25	10–13	32
Washington	5–7	2–2	12	B. Jones	8–11	3–4	19
Johnson	3–4	2–2	8	C. Jones	4–7	1–1	9
Money	11–16	1–2	23	Cheeks	1–6	0–0	2
Williamson	14–21	6–6	34	Collins	3–10	4–4	10
Elliott	0–1	0–0	0	Bibby	3–6	5–6	11
Boynes	1–3	0–0	2	Dawkins	6–0	1–2	13
V. Breda Kolff	5–8	2–4	12	Mix	3–9	3–4	9
Jordan	1–4	4–6	6	Simpson	4–6	0–0	8
Bassett	0–0	0–0	0	Bryant	3–7	0–0	6
Skinner	Did Not Play			Catchings	0–1	0–0	0
Catchings	2–4	4–4	8	Skinner	Did Not Play		
Simpson	0–0	0–0	0	Money	2–4	0–0	4
Jackson	2–7	0–0	4				
Totals	**47–86**	**23–28**	**117**	**Totals**	**48–101**	**27–34**	**123**

New Jersey	38	32	29	18	—	**117**
Philadelphia	21	41	34	27	—	**123**

Rebounds: Philadelphia 45 (B. Jones 9), New Jersey 44 (Johnson 10); Assists: Philadelphia 35 (Erving, Bibby 8), New Jersey 25 (Jordan 6); Steals: Philadelphia 10 (Collins, B. Jones 2), New Jersey 9 (Van Breda Kolff 3); Blocked Shots: New Jersey 13 (Johnson 8), Philadelphia 5 (Erving, B. Jones 2); Officials: Earl Strom, Bill Saar, Jack Madden; T: 2:00. A: 11,368.

HOCKEY

Gretzky's Great Moment

Wayne Gretzky has always been called "The Great One," or "The Great Gretzky." From his days growing up in Brantford, Ontario, playing peewee and midget hockey, he always seemed to be in a league by himself, scoring seemingly at will.

But Gretzky's greatest thrill as a youngster was not scoring goals or setting records; instead, it was meeting his idol, Gordie Howe, at a dinner following one of Wayne's record-breaking seasons. At the time, Howe was finishing up a career in which he had rewritten much of the NHL record books. He was the league's all-time leader in goals and points, but Howe had no idea that night that he was meeting his successor.

Gordie Howe congratulates Wayne Gretzky on record-breaking night.

Gretzky had started playing professional hockey at the age of 17, and in his first nine seasons in the NHL he won eight scoring titles and paced the Edmonton Oilers to four Stanley Cups. He was traded to the Los Angeles Kings in 1988 in the biggest hockey trade of all time, but the change of teams did nothing to slow down his quest for Howe's scoring record of 1,850 points.

Going into the 1989–90 season, Gretzky had 1,837 points. In the first two weeks, Gretzky had climbed within one point of the record, and ironically, the Kings' next game was scheduled in Edmonton, where Gretzky was still regarded as a hero. The crowd at Northlands Coliseum on October 15, 1989, was divided, wanting Gretzky to set the record but rooting for the Oilers.

In the first period, Gretzky got an assist to tie Howe's mark. But he was shut out from then on until the game came down to the final minute, with the Oilers leading, 4–3. The Kings kept the puck in the offensive zone and Gretzky stood behind the net, waiting for his chance. Suddenly, the Kings' Dave Taylor got the puck along the right boards and sent a pass toward the net. Gretzky reacted quickly, skating out from behind the net and deflecting the puck past Oilers goalie Bill Ranford. The record was his!

Fittingly, Howe was at the game and one of the first to congratulate Gretzky when the game was halted to celebrate the occasion. "In all honesty, I've been looking forward to today," said Howe, whose record had been set over 26 seasons.

Gretzky, who needed only 11 seasons to surpass Howe, was his usual modest self. "Gordie is still the greatest," he said.

And with that, the game resumed. And The Great Gretzky proceeded to score in overtime to give the Kings the victory.

Oh, Brother!

Bryan Murray got the bad news on January 15, 1990.

Minutes later, Terry Murray got the good news.

Bryan was fired as coach of the Washington Capitals.

Terry was hired as coach of the Washington Capitals.

They are brothers!

Bryan had coached the Capitals since 1981–82, and the team was in the throes of an eight-game losing streak.

Terry was coach of the Washington affiliate, the Baltimore Skipjacks in the American League.

Said Bryan: "I'm disappointed for myself, but I'm happy for Terry."

Goalie on the Shoot

NHL goaltenders are not where they are because of their ability to shoot the puck. Reflexes, guts and skating ability are what most scouts look for when rating a goalie. The Philadelphia Flyers' Ron Hextall added another dimension.

Hextall grew up in a hockey family. His

grandfather Bryan scored the winning goal in overtime to give the Rangers the Stanley Cup in 1940, and his father, Bryan, Jr., and his uncle Dennis were rugged performers in the 1960s.

But while his relatives were all forwards, Ron decided at a young age he would rather be a goalie. His father insisted, however, that Ron practice his skating and shooting as well as his goaltending so that if Ron ever changed his mind and decided to try another position, he would be ready.

But Ron never changed his mind, and his goaltending was good enough in junior hockey to earn him a spot with the Philadelphia Flyers in the 1986–87 season. Soon after he joined the club he told a reporter that he would like to be the first NHL goaltender to score a goal.

He knew that the Islanders' Billy Smith had received credit for a goal years before, but Smith had not actually shot the puck into the net. A Colorado player had inadvertently put the puck in, but Smith had been the last Islander to touch the puck and was given credit.

Hextall wanted to be the first to actually shoot a puck into the net. The Flyers would have to have a lead in the closing minutes of a game, and the opposition would have to have pulled its goalie to get an extra skater on ice.

On December 8, 1987, at the Spectrum in Philadelphia, the Flyers were leading the Bruins, 4–2, in the final minute and Boston goalie Rejean Lemelin was on the bench. The Bruins' Gord Kluzak took a shot that Hextall stopped behind the goal. Suddenly, Hextall controlled the puck, turned, and wristed a shot over the approaching Bruins. The puck bounced in center ice and slid straight down the ice into the Bruins' net.

Hextall will always be remembered for being the first NHL goalie to shoot a puck into an opposing goal.

One-Man Show

Mario Lemieux wasn't feeling well, but he knew his team needed him. It was Game 5 of the 1989 Patrick Division finals, and Lemieux's Pittsburgh Penguins were tied with the Philadelphia Flyers at two games apiece. The Penguins needed desperately to win the fifth game; if they lost, they would be behind, 3–2, and the Flyers would need only to win Game 6 at home to finish the series.

The Penguins' hopes were dimmed by an injury to Lemieux in Game 4. Mario had collided with teammate Randy Cunneyworth and had suffered a neck injury that made it difficult to turn his head. Without Lemieux, the NHL's scoring leader for two seasons and the man who had scored an incredible 282 points in 70 games in his final season of junior hockey, the Penguins would be out of it.

Hours before gametime, Lemieux decided he would try to play. His night got off to a good start when, just 2:15 into the first period, he picked up a loose puck at center ice, went in alone on a breakaway and beat Flyers goalie Ron Hextall. Less than two minutes later, Lemieux was standing at the side of the net when teammate Bob Errey fed him a perfect pass. Lemieux beat Hextall again and suddenly it was 2–0.

A few minutes later, the Penguins were on a power play when Lemieux got the puck on the right side of the Flyers' goal, skated into the right face-off circle and fired a shot that went between Hextall's pads. Later in the period, Hextall went behind his net to stop a puck. In a flash, Lemieux streaked in, stole the puck from the goalie and stuffed in a wrap-around shot before Hextall could scramble back into the net. Lemieux's fourth goal of the period tied a playoff record set by the Flyers' Tim Kerr against the Rangers in 1985.

But Lemieux wasn't through yet. He assisted on three Pittsburgh goals in the second period and then capped off a magnificent effort with an empty-net goal after the Flyers, trailing 9–7, pulled Hextall in the final minute of the third period. Five goals, three assists, and the Penguins won, 10–7. Lemieux's eight points in a playoff game tied a record set by the Devils' Patrik Sundstrom against Washington in 1988.

"It was a big night," Lemieux said.

Imagine what he could have done if he'd felt better.

The Endless Game

The New York Islanders and the Washington Capitals had no idea what they were getting into when they took the ice at Landover, Maryland, on Saturday, April 18, 1987. Since it was Game 7 of the Patrick Division semifinals, they knew one team would survive while the other would stash away its gear for the summer. What they didn't know was how long it would take to determine a winner.

Mike Gartner tipped in a shot with 48 seconds left in the first period to give Washington a 1–0 lead, but midway through the second period a goal by Patrick Flatley got the Islanders even. The first sign that this was no ordinary night came in the closing minutes of the period when the Capitals' Grant Martin, who had not scored in any of his previous 44 NHL games, beat Islanders goalie Kelly Hrudey with a short shot to give the Capitals a 2–1 lead.

Washington controlled the third period until playoff veteran Bryan Trottier took a pass from Alan Kerr and backhanded a shot through goalie Bob Mason's pads, tying the game with 5:23 left in the third period. Neither team could score in regulation time, so the teams headed for sudden-death overtime, where one goal would end it all.

The teams played one 20-minute overtime period. And then another. And still another. But both goalies were brilliant and when they weren't, shots were clanging off goal posts. Finally, in the fourth overtime, Islanders center Pat LaFontaine picked up a loose puck 40 feet in front of Mason, turned and fired a shot that hit off the right goal post and deflected into the net. At 1:56 A.M. on Easter Sunday morning, more than six hours after the game started, the Islanders had won, 3–2.

It was the longest NHL game in 44 years and the fifth-longest of all time.

Old Man in the Nets

It was Game 2 of the 1928 Stanley Cup finals between the New York Rangers and the Montreal Maroons.

Montreal's Nels Stewart drilled a blistering shot that hit goalie Lorne Chabot in the left eye and knocked him unconscious.

In those days, a team usually had only one goalie, so a replacement would have to be someone other than a goalie. As Ranger coach Lester Patrick pondered a replacement, center Frank Boucher half-jokingly asked: "How about you?"

Patrick was 45 and long removed from his playing days as a defenseman. But he responded by climbing into Chabot's blood-stained equipment.

Patrick was trembling as he went into the nets and blocked a few easy practice shots. When the scoreless game resumed, the Rangers played like a team possessed. They made the New York zone a no-man's land for the Maroons as they protected their white-haired leader.

Patrick stopped everything shot his way in the extra period, and at 7:05 Boucher scored the winning goal. Now the series was tied at

1-all. Later, armed with a real goalie, they went on to win the Stanley Cup. But it was the old man in the nets who had supplied the inspiration.

An aging Lester Patrick emerged as a goalie.

BOXING

Hypnosis in the Ring

Dr. Michael Dean, a hypnotist, began treating heavyweight boxer Ken Norton after he was knocked out by José Luis Garcia in 1970.

"My backers felt I wasn't prepared mentally or physically. They urged me to see this hypnotist," Norton said.

Norton and Dr. Dean had a number of sessions over the next three years before Norton took his 28–1 record into the ring against heavyweight champion Muhammad Ali on March 31, 1973.

Norton was a 5–1 underdog in the bout at the San Diego Sports Arena. But in the biggest fight of his life, he broke Ali's jaw and won a split 12-round decision. And he credited the hypnotist — who taught him to relax, among

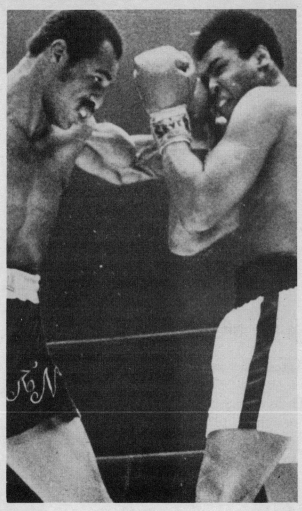

Ken Norton unloads against Muhammad Ali in their first bout.

other things — with playing an important role in the triumph.

But where was the hypnotist three months later when Ali decisioned Norton in a 12-round rematch?

Mama's Boy

It happened in the third round of the welterweight match between Tony Wilson and Steve McCarthy at Southhampton, England, on September 21, 1988.

Minna Wilson, Tony's mother, climbed into the ring and beat her son's opponent over the head with her shoe. She opened a cut on McCarthy's head. At the time, McCarthy had Wilson pinned against the ropes.

McCarthy left the ring and required four stitches. He refused to continue the fight, and the decision was awarded to Wilson.

The British Boxing Board of Control upheld the ruling but ordered a rematch.

"I don't know what happened to me," said Minna Wilson, who claimed that she had been upset by the crowd's racial slurs toward her son, who is black. "I'm really sorry."

Wilson's manager, Jimmy Tibbs, said: "She did what any mum would do under the circumstances."

"She's been watching my fights for years and nothing like this has ever happened before," Wilson said.

He barred his mum from ever attending any of his future fights.

Ingemar's Burden

His countrymen in Sweden had high hopes for Ingemar Johansson as he faced America's Eddie Sanders in the heavyweight boxing final at the 1952 Olympic Games in Helsinki, Finland.

From the beginning of the bout, however, Johansson kept retreating. The referee warned Ingemar several times, but when his backtracking continued in the second round, the referee disqualified Johansson for "not trying" and awarded the title to Sanders.

Olympic officials refused to give Johansson the silver medal for second place, and even the Swedish newspapers were critical of him. One headline read: "For Shame, Ingemar."

But that was not the end of Johansson's boxing career. He turned professional and on June 26, 1959, the boxer who hadn't been aggressive knocked out Floyd Patterson to win the world heavyweight championship at New York's Yankee Stadium.

Power-punching Ingemar Johansson finds his mark against Floyd Patterson in championship fight.

A year later, Patterson would knock out Johansson to regain his title. Whatever his professional accomplishments, Johansson would have to live forever with the stigma of that Olympic final when, as one reporter wrote, "he ran for his life."

OLYMPICS

Matching His Idol

The world's eyes were focused on a gentle and soft-spoken track star during the 1984 Summer Olympics in Los Angeles. And for good reason. Carl Lewis was hoping to become the first American athlete since the legendary Jesse Owens in 1936 to win four Olympic gold medals in track and field.

As a youngster growing up in Willingboro, New Jersey, Lewis came from an athletic family. His parents were track coaches at rival high schools. His mother, Evelyn, had been an outstanding hurdler in the 1950s. And Carl's sister, Carol, his closest friend and confidante,

Carl Lewis heads for the gold medal at 200 meters in the 1984 Olympic Games in Los Angeles.

was a world-class long jumper.

But Carl had found his inspiration in Jesse Owens, whom he had met when he was 12 at a youth track program.

At the Olympics, Lewis began his historic pursuit of his hero in grand style. He won the 100-meter dash in a blazing 9.9 seconds, immediately laying claim to the title, "World's Fastest Human." The crowd in the Los Angeles Coliseum roared as Lewis borrowed an American flag from a spectator and waved it triumphantly.

The next evening, Lewis told a teammate that if he felt right, he would go for the world long jump record set by America's Bob Beamon in 1968. In his first jump, Lewis sprinted down the runway, accelerating to a speed of 27 miles an hour, and took off. He landed at 28¼ feet — an excellent jump, but short of Beamon's 29-2½ record.

Confident that he had clinched a gold medal, Lewis passed on his final four jumps, saying, "I got a little sore and didn't want to risk the chance of injury." But the crowd — the same people who cheered his first gold medal in the 100-meter dash — booed his second. They wanted to see Lewis try for the record.

"I was shocked at first," Lewis said. "But

after I thought about it, I realized they were booing because they wanted to see more of Carl Lewis. I guess that's flattering."

In the 200-meter dash, he blazed to an Olympic record of 19.80 seconds for his third gold medal.

But perhaps Carl saved his best for last. He and three American teammates set an Olympic record by running the 400-meter relay in a stunning 37.83 seconds. Carl, running the anchor leg, hit the tape more than 20 feet ahead of Jamaica's Ray Stewart.

Lewis had fulfilled his goal of four gold medals, duplicating the feat of his role model and idol, Jesse Owens.

Foiled!

The Soviet Union's Boris Onischenko had been a silver medalist in the modern pentathlon at the 1972 Olympic Games in Munich, West Germany. He was a leading contender for honors again at the 1976 Olympics in Montreal.

Dueling in the fencing event, his opponent, England's Jeremy Fox, jumped back without being touched. But Onischenko's épée (sword) registered a hit. Fox protested and following an investigation, Onischenko was disqualified.

The officials detected a bugging device in his épée — a button hidden in the handle which, when pressed, set off the electronic signal indicating a hit.

As a result, Onischenko not only lost his chance for a medal, he came home to a cool reception in the USSR. He was given a lesser job and he was ousted from the athletic clubs where he'd trained over the years.

Doing What He Oerter

As a schoolboy, Al Oerter started competing in the 100-yard dash. As he grew bigger he tried the mile, but by the time he became a 200-pounder he found the object of his affection — the discus. He would propel it and himself to Olympian heights.

As a 20-year-old sophomore at Kansas University, he made the U.S. Olympic team and won the gold medal with a record 184-foot, 11-inch toss at the 1956 Olympic Games in Melbourne, Australia.

In 1960, by then a 6-foot-4, 275-pounder, he won gold again with a record 194–2 at the Olympics in Rome. Despite a rib injury and a

Record-setting Al Oerter flings the discus at the 1968 Olympic Games in Mexico City.

neck ailment, he made it three Olympic golds in a row with a record toss of 200–1 at Tokyo in 1964.

In 1968, at age 32, he did it again at the Mexico City Olympics — a record 212–6 and his fourth straight gold medal.

He thus became the only athlete to have won four golds in the same event in separate Games. It's a record that still stands.

A Diving Team

Divers Betty Becker and Clarence Pinkston were among the 300 U.S. athletes and officials on the SS *America* when it embarked from New York for Paris and the 1924 Olympic Games. Aboard ship the swimmers had a small canvas tank, and the runners worked out on a 220-yard cork track. But, short of sampling the Atlantic, the divers couldn't practice their specialty.

It didn't hurt their performance in Paris, however. Betty Becker won a gold medal in the springboard event, and Clarence Pinkston took bronze in both the platform and springboard.

A shipboard romance blossomed and they got married after the Olympics. The Pinkstons were known henceforth as the first couple to win Olympic medals in the same sport.

Eric Heiden rockets to his first gold medal in the 500-meter race in the 1980 Olympic Games at Lake Placid, N.Y.

Blades of Gold

In the Netherlands he was called the "God of Speed Skating," while in Norway he was a national hero, a young man whose face was on cartons of milk and whose praises were sung in a song. But in his own country, the United States, Eric Heiden was a relative stranger participating in an obscure sport. This was until the 1980 Winter Olympics at Lake Placid, New York, transformed Heiden into the All-American boy.

He was a 21-year-old premed student from Madison, Wisconsin, and he'd devoted four years preceding the Olympics to reach his full potential.

Displaying the strength and speed needed to win at the shorter distances, as well as the stamina required in the marathon events, Heiden reeled off gold-medal performances at 500 meters, 1,000, 1,500, and 5,000 and saved his best for the last, breaking the world record by six seconds in winning the 10,000-meter race in 14:28:13.

It all added up to five gold medals, the most anyone had ever won in the same Winter Games.

GOLF

Aces High

The grounds at Oak Hill Country Club in Pittsford, New York — site of the 1989 U.S. Open Golf tournament — were softened by several days of rain. But lightning struck on the second round. Actually, lightning struck four times.

On the par-three, 167-yard sixth hole, Doug Weaver drove a tee shot that hit a small slope 15 feet from the pin. The ball spun back and gently rolled in for a hole-in-one.

It was a singular achievement, considering that the odds of a hole-in-one by a pro golfer in a single round were calculated at 3,708 to 1.

Yet not even a Las Vegas oddsmaker could calculate the odds against four golfers using the same club — a 7 iron — making a hole-in-one at the same hole in the U.S. Open.

But that's what happened. After Weaver's ace, Mark Wiebe landed his tee shot into the cup. And so did Jerry Pate and Nick Price.

"It was," Wiebe said, "one of those fluky things."

It had never happened before and probably will never happen again — not at the same sixth hole by four golfers using the same club.

"There won't be any more holes-in-one there," said John Morse of the Professional Golfers Association. "We're planting a tree there."

Recovery of the Day

Mary Bea Porter was lining up her shot on the 13th fairway of the Moon Valley Country Club in Phoenix, Arizona, when she saw the little boy.

He'd just been pulled out, face down, from a swimming pool by his father, but Mary Bea realized that the parents didn't know how to revive the lad.

She instantly dropped her golf club, climbed over a six-foot fence and performed mouth-to-mouth resuscitation. The three-year-old boy,

Jonathan Smucker, was crying in her arms when paramedics arrived. All was well.

But not for Mary Bea, who was trying to qualify for the *Standard-Register* Turquoise Classic. Shaken, she returned to the golf course, bogeyed two of the next three holes, and finished with a 76. That meant she missed qualifying by three strokes. So what?

Well, 30 golfers from the Ladies Professional Golf Association signed a petition requesting that, under the circumstances, she be made a qualifier. And she got to compete in the Turquoise Classic.

What's more, her lifesaving feat inspired creation of the Mary Bea Porter Humanitarian Award, which is given annually to golfers who make singular contributions away from the fairway.

EQUESTRIAN

Out of Sight!

Tori Watters has won her share of blue ribbons in the jumper class at horse shows from Florida to Lake Placid, New York.

Sports commentator Bob Wolff interviewed her while covering the 1987 National Horse Show at New York City's Madison Square Garden. He called the 23-year-old rider from Cincinnati "one of the most remarkable athletes" he'd met in more than 40 years of broadcasting.

Tori Watters is blind.

She lost her sight after undergoing surgery for a brain tumor when she was 14.

How does she negotiate the course with its assorted jumps?

"My trainer tells me how many strides there are between the fences," she said. "He describes the fence; if it's a wide fence, I need to ride up to it some to let my horse get over it. He tells me if it's going to be 'spooky.' My horse is a young horse, so if it's spooky, I need to be a little stronger in my ride."

On the course she sees the image of the jumps as little blurs. She has been hospitalized by falls, but she always returns to the saddle.

Her horse is named Out of Sight.

Dancing Hooves

She'd once been an aspiring actress, but for more than a decade she'd become accustomed to the sound of hoofbeats as she traveled from one race track to another. Robyn Smith was a pioneer among the women jockeys, one of the first female riders.

But in the summer of 1980, the 35-year-old Smith said she was giving up the hoofbeats for the love of a famous hoofer. She married 80-year-old Fred Astaire, the famous American dancer and movie star.

Chocolate Bars Horses

De Rigueur, a four-year-old gelding, munched on a chocolate bar before he won the Balmoral Handicap at England's Ascot race course in September 1987.

But the Jockey Club, governing body of British horse-racing, ruled that the chocolate bar contained a prohibited stimulant called theobromine. It showed up in De Rigueur's urine test. The horse was disqualified, its owner losing $15,000 in prize money.

Trainer James Bethell, who was fined $860, said he didn't blame 17-year-old stable girl Tanya Mayne, who admitted feeding the horse the candy bar. "All horses like sweet things," Bethell said. "I'm not surprised he ate the bar."

Michael Chang stole the show in the 1989 French Open.

TENNIS

Cheers for Chang

The French Open is one of the premier tournaments in tennis. But it had been a curse for Americans. For 34 years, not one U.S. male — not even such stars as John McEnroe and Jimmy Connors — could win on the red clay courts in Paris.

The 1989 French Open gave little hint of a change.

One of America's hopes was a slightly built 17-year-old high-school kid, but he seemed hopelessly overmatched early in the tournament. His name was Michael Chang, and when he faced Ivan Lendl of Czechoslovakia, the world's top-ranked player, in an early round, he suffered leg cramps. Somehow, Chang played through the pain and managed to upset the great Lendl. Later, battling mounting fatigue, Chang collapsed on the court minutes after defeating Soviet Andrei Chesnokov in the semifinals.

The experts felt it would take nothing short of a miracle in the finals for him to overcome Sweden's Stefan Edberg, an experienced pro with a superior volley and winner of three of tennis' major tournaments.

Michael's father had faith, if few others did. "Even when he was seven years old, Michael was a fighter," Joe Chang said. "He's always had the heart and mind to be a champion."

When the match began, Michael appeared to tire early. His forehand was failing. Perhaps it was the strain of an exhausting week under scorching temperatures. Perhaps the pressure of playing before 16,500 spectators had an effect, too.

But Michael never gave up. "To tell the truth," he said, "I don't know what kept me going."

And the youngster from Placentia, California, eventually wore down Edberg. "He kept missing shots," Chang said. "I kept making them. He gave me an opening, and once he did I said to myself, 'Hey, you can do this.' "

After a grueling three hours and 41 minutes,

Chang defeated Edberg, 6–1, 3–6, 4–6, 6–4, 6–2.

Not only was Michael — his dad is from China and his mother is Taiwanese — the only American since Tony Trabert in 1955 to win the French Open, he was also the youngest.

"Whatever happens from now on, good or bad," Michael said, "this will stay with me the rest of my life."

Making a Point

They weren't trying for a record. In the course of a 1984 Virginia Slims tennis match, Vicki Nelson-Dunbar and Jean Hepner engaged in a volley that turned into a marathon.

It lasted 29 minutes and the ball was hit 643 times before the point was scored. Nelson-Dunbar eventually won the match, 6–4, 7–6, (13–11), but its significance is that it was the longest-recorded volley in the history of tennis.

For 16-year-old Tracy Austin, this was the big one against Chris Evert at the 1979 U.S. Open.

Sweet 16

She had been hitting tennis balls since she was an infant. She was on the cover of *World Tennis* magazine at age four, and on the cover of *Sports Illustrated* at age 13.

And now, 16-year-old Tracy Austin of Rolling Hills, California, was in the 1979 U.S. Open final against 24-year-old Chris Evert at Flushing Meadow, New York.

Evert had won the title four times and had reigned over women's tennis from the baseline, with patience and perseverance. And it was the finalists' similarity in style and single-mindedness that made this a perfect matchup.

There was Austin, racing from one side of the baseline to the other, hitting a two-fisted backhand, driving a forehand to the alley. Several times Evert thought she had a winner, only to see the ball come back at her. Or past her.

Early in the match the cheers of the more than 18,000 spectators had been for the defending champion, but now there were increasing calls of "Let's go, Tracy!"

And the California schoolgirl responded by dethroning Evert, 6–4, 6–3. At 16, she became the youngest U.S. Open Champion ever.